SandCastle™

Sports
By the Numbers

# Skateboarding
## By the Numbers

**Desirée Bussiere**

Consulting Editor, Diane Craig, M.A./Reading Specialist

A Division of ABDO

**ABDO**
Publishing Company

# visit us at www.abdopublishing.com

Published by ABDO Publishing Company, a division of ABDO, P.O. Box 398166, Minneapolis, Minnesota 55439. Copyright © 2014 by Abdo Consulting Group, Inc. International copyrights reserved in all countries. No part of this book may be reproduced in any form without written permission from the publisher. SandCastle™ is a trademark and logo of ABDO Publishing Company.

Printed in the United States of America, North Mankato, Minnesota
062013
092013

 PRINTED ON RECYCLED PAPER

Editor: Liz Salzmann
Content Developer: Nancy Tuminelly
Cover and Interior Design and Production: Colleen Dolphin, Mighty Media
Cover Production: Kate Hartman
Photo Credits: Shutterstock, Thinkstock

Library of Congress Cataloging-in-Publication Data

Bussiere, Desiree, 1989-
  Skateboarding by the numbers / Desiree Bussiere.
     pages cm. -- (Sports by the numbers)
  ISBN 978-1-61783-845-3
1. Skateboarding--Juvenile literature. I. Title.
  GV859.8.B88 2014
  796.22--dc23
                          2012049957

## SandCastle™ Level: Transitional

SandCastle™ books are created by a team of professional educators, reading specialists, and content developers around five essential components—phonemic awareness, phonics, vocabulary, text comprehension, and fluency—to assist young readers as they develop reading skills and strategies and increase their general knowledge. All books are written, reviewed, and leveled for guided reading, early reading intervention, and Accelerated Reader® programs for use in shared, guided, and independent reading and writing activities to support a balanced approach to literacy instruction. The SandCastle™ series has four levels that correspond to early literacy development. The levels are provided to help teachers and parents select appropriate books for young readers.

| Emerging Readers | Beginning Readers | Transitional Readers | Fluent Readers |
| (no flags) | (1 flag) | (2 flags) | (3 flags) |

# Contents

# Introduction

Numbers are used all the time in skateboarding.

- Skate park **obstacles** are usually 50 feet (15 m) **apart**.

- Skateboard wheels are 2 to 4 inches (5 to 10 cm) across.

- The mega **ramp** used in the X Games is 9 stories tall.

- Skaters can reach up to 15 miles per hour (24 kph) on a 6-foot (2 m) mini-ramp.

Let's learn more about how numbers are used in skateboarding.

# The Skate Park

30 feet
(9.1 m)

50 feet
(15.2 m)

20 feet
(6.1 m)

# The Sport

Facing 2 **ramps** together forms a half-pipe.

There are 2 main types of skateboarding. They are street and vert skating.

Most tricks have 4 to 6 steps.

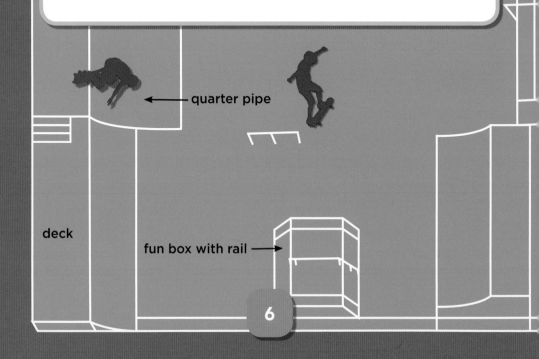

quarter pipe

deck

fun box with rail

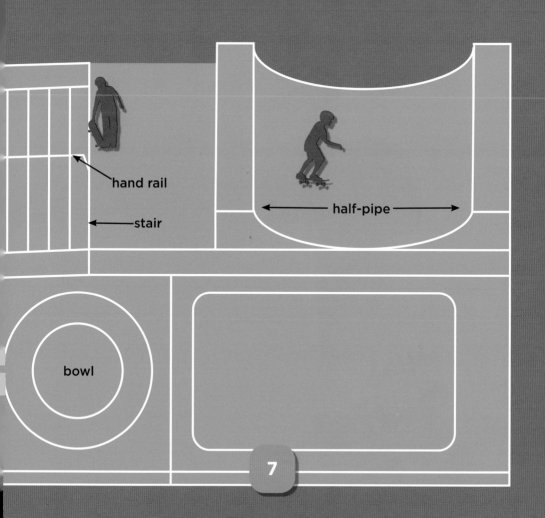

hand rail

stair

half-pipe

bowl

8

Anna loves to ride her skateboard. Her brother Tom taught her how.

## By the Numbers!

**A** Anna first tried skateboarding when she was 7. She has been doing it for 3 years. How old is she now?

*(answer on p. 23)*

Danny rolls off the
mini-**ramp**. It is his **favorite**!

## By the Numbers!

**B**

Danny skated down the ramp 10 times today. Yesterday he went down it 8 times. How many more times did he go down the ramp today?

*(answer on p. 23)*

Aaron and Maddy are racing. The first one over the mini-**ramp** gets 4 points.

## By the Numbers!

C Maddy jumped the ramp first! Now she has 8 points. Aaron has 4 points. How many more points does Maddy have?

*(answer on p. 23)*

14

Christy likes to ride her skateboard after school.

## By the Numbers!

**D**

Christy skated 3 days last week. She skated 2 days this week. How many days did she skate total?

*(answer on p. 23)*

Mike does tricks in the half-pipe.

**E** Mike does 1 trick on one side of the pipe. He does 3 tricks on the other side. How many tricks does he do?

*(answer on p. 23)*

18

# Katie skates the half pipe.

## By the Numbers!

**F**

Katie does 9 tricks. She only gets points for 6 of them. How many tricks aren't counted?

*(answer on p. 23)*

Jake is at the skateboard park. He goes after school.

By the Numbers!

G

Jake rides 5 rails. He jumps 4 fun boxes. How many **obstacles** does he skate on?

(answer on p. 23)

# Skateboarding Facts

- Danny Wainwright did the highest **ollie** ever. It was 44.5 inches (113 cm) high!

- Tony Hawk did the first 900-**degree** spin in midair. That's two and a half spins.

- Danny Way jumped his skateboard over the Great Wall of China. He did it 5 times in one day.

- At the X Games, skaters fly down an 80-foot (24 m) **ramp**. They do tricks to earn points.

- The flat part of a skateboard is called a deck. A deck has 7 pieces of wood.

# Answers to By the Numbers!

**D**

$$3$$
$$+2$$
$$\overline{\phantom{0}5\phantom{0}}$$

Christy skated 3 days last week. She skated 2 days this week. How many days did she skate total?

**A**

$$7$$
$$+3$$
$$\overline{10}$$

Anna first tried skateboarding when she was 7. She has been doing it for 3 years. How old is she now?

**E**

$$1$$
$$+3$$
$$\overline{\phantom{0}4\phantom{0}}$$

Mike does 1 trick on one side of the pipe. He does 3 tricks on the other side. How many tricks does he do?

**B**

$$10$$
$$-8$$
$$\overline{\phantom{0}2\phantom{0}}$$

Danny skated down the **ramp** 10 times today. Yesterday he went down it 8 times. How many more times did he go down the ramp today?

**F**

$$9$$
$$-6$$
$$\overline{\phantom{0}3\phantom{0}}$$

Katie does 9 tricks. She only gets points for 6 of them. How many tricks aren't counted?

**C**

$$8$$
$$-4$$
$$\overline{\phantom{0}4\phantom{0}}$$

Maddy jumped the ramp first! Now she has 8 points. Aaron has 4 points. How many more points does Maddy have?

**G**

$$5$$
$$+4$$
$$\overline{\phantom{0}9\phantom{0}}$$

Jake rides 5 rails. He jumps 4 fun boxes. How many **obstacles** does he skate on?

23

# Glossary

**apart** – away from each other.

**degree** – a unit used to measure how far something turns. One complete turn is 360 degrees.

**favorite** – someone or something that you like best.

**obstacle** – something that you have to go over or around.

**ollie** – a trick in which the skater pushes the back of the skateboard down to make it jump in the air.

**ramp** – a lane or path that slopes up or down.